Killer Whales

ANIMAL PREDATORS

SANDRA MARKLE

Carolrhoda Books, Inc. / Minneapolis

THE ANIMAL WORLD IS FULL OF
PREDATORS.

Predators are the hunters who find, catch, and eat other animals—their prey—in order to survive. Every environment has its chain of hunters. The smaller, slower, less able predators become prey for the bigger, faster, more cunning hunters. And everywhere, there are just a few kinds of predators at the top of the food chain. *In the oceans of the world, one of these is the orca, also called the killer whale.*

Killer whales are successful predators because they usually hunt in a group called a pod. Sometimes a pod is a group of males that hunts together. Sometimes it's a family of hunters made up of a lead female, her children, and her grandchildren. Unlike lions and wolves, who fight over pieces of the prey, killer whales in a pod share every meal.

Killer whales have keen senses to help them find prey such as fish, sharks, and seals. The killer whale may first learn that prey is nearby through its ears. The whale's lower jawbone works like an antenna. The jawbone picks up sound waves traveling through the water and transmits them to the whale's ears. A killer whale also produces pulses of clicking sounds. These clicks bounce off fish and other objects in the water. The whale's brain analyzes the returning echoes of these clicks and creates a sound picture of the killer whale's underwater world.

This female killer whale is spyhopping—pushing her head above the water—to look for prey on the surface of the sea. Each eye works separately, so she can quickly scan a large area on each side of her head. The other killer whales with her look too. When one of the young females spots a seal resting on an ice floe—a floating piece of ice—she signals with a burst of clicks. Then she slips underwater and the others follow.

Killer whales can swim fast when they choose to. An adult killer whale can swim as fast as 35 miles per hour (56 kilometers per hour).

Breaching, or leaping from the water, helps a killer whale pick up speed. That's because every time it's in the air, the whale is free of the water's pull on its body.

As they swim closer to the seal, the hunters' dark backs help them hide in the dark ocean water. Then the pod splits up, encircling the seal on the ice floe.

Suddenly, the lead female uses her tail to push a wave of water over the ice floe. The wave washes the seal off the floe. When the seal lands in the sea, the closest killer whale attacks.

To catch prey, a killer whale is armed with a whole mouthful of weapons—more than forty big teeth. Each tooth is about 3 inches (8 centimeters) long and is very sharp.

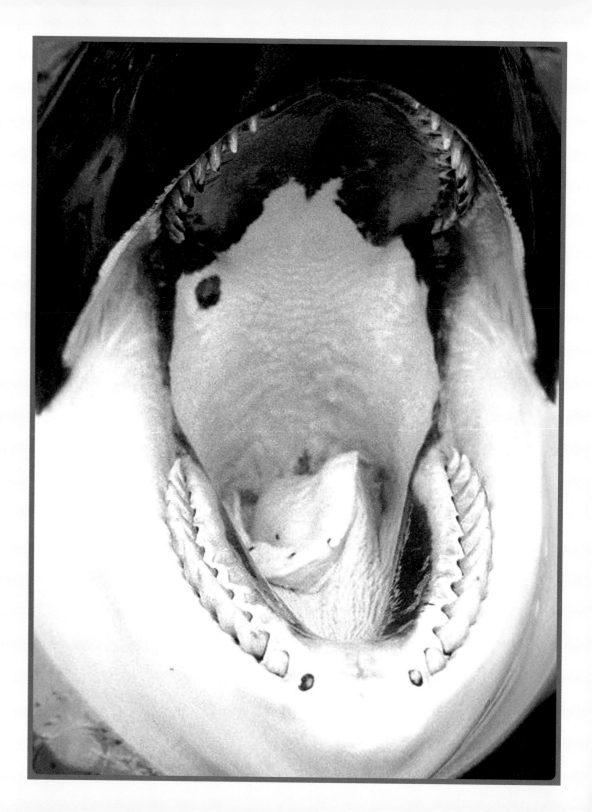

The seal has one advantage, though. Being smaller, it can turn faster than the big predator. This time, the seal is able to twist so quickly that it escapes with just a gash across its head. Before the hunter can open its mouth and bite again, the seal rushes ashore.

Meanwhile, still hungry, the pod swims away to search again for a meal. As they swim, the members of the pod stay close to the surface. Killer whales live in the water, but they breathe air through a blowhole on top of their heads. A flap closes this opening between breaths and when the killer whales are under water.

It doesn't take long for the pod to find another seal. The killer whales close
in from all sides to try to keep this prey from getting away.

Then the adults hold back to give a young female, the youngest member of the pod, a chance to practice her hunting skills. While the adults click and squeak, the young hunter chases the seal. When her prey leaps out of the water, the female jumps too. She bites, but misses. The seal swims away quickly. Then it sees one of the adult killer whales straight ahead. The seal veers toward the surface again.

This time when the seal leaps, the young female's timing is better. Her powerful jaws snap shut just in time to snatch the seal. After making the kill, the young hunter gets the first bite of meat. Then the young hunter shares what she has caught. Pod members don't have to waste energy competing for food.

Satisfied for the moment, the killer whales are ready to play. The youngster chases two adults until they breach. For a few seconds, the killer whales soar gracefully and fall back to the water. Then, just for fun, one giant twists and flops on its back, making a big splash.

Later, the killer whales nap. Like all animals, killer whales need to sleep. Sometimes they rest clustered all together at the surface. This time, they take their naps while they are swimming. Like many kinds of whales, killer whales sleep by resting half of their brains. The other half remains awake and in control of their bodies' activities.

Closer to shore, another pod is about to have a herring dinner. The lead female twists her body, flashing her white belly at the school of fish. Alarmed, the herring flee in the opposite direction. But another member of the pod is waiting for them. This killer whale also flashes its white belly. The startled fish dive, only to find yet another hunter below them. This killer whale drives the fish upward. There, waiting killer whales slap the fish with their broad tail fins called flukes. This stuns and kills many of the herring.

Finally, the pod joins together to feed. A killer whale's throat is divided into separate tubes. One tube is for swallowing food and leads to the stomach. The other tube is for breathing and leads to the lungs. The pod members communicate in trills, grunts, clicks, and squeaks while they eat.

It's easy to spot the male killer whales in a pod. The male's tall dorsal fin on his back stands much taller than the female's dorsal fin. A male's fin can be as tall as some professional basketball players. Sometimes male killer whales travel alone. They may join a pod only to mate. Sometimes two or more pods may hunt together. Then the males and females from the two different pods mate.

This little female developed inside her mother's body for almost sixteen months. When she is ready to be born, the calf slips out of her mother tailfirst into the cold sea.

She's a big baby—more than 8 feet (2 meters) long. She weighs about 400 pounds (180 kilograms). Because the newborn whale can't swim very well, her mother helps her to the surface. As soon as the baby's blowhole is above the water, she takes her first breath.

The newborn dives, searching for the nipples tucked into a slit on her mother's belly. When she finds one, she nudges but doesn't suck. Sucking would pull in seawater. Instead, her mother's muscles squeeze, squirting milk down the baby's throat.

Unable to hold her breath for long, the newborn feeds for only about one minute before surfacing. She'll nurse as often as twenty times an hour for the first few weeks. A killer whale's milk is nearly half fat, thicker than dairy cream. This will help the calf grow bigger fast. She'll also develop a thick layer of her own fat, called blubber. This will help the calf stay warm in the cold ocean.

In about two months, the calf's upper teeth come in. In about two more months, she gets her bottom teeth. After that, her family begins to share bits of solid food with her. But the youngster continues to nurse for two years.

During her early years, the little calf learns how to talk to her pod. At first, the baby's calls are shrill screams. But she mimics the sounds her mother makes. Finally she's able to produce the same trills, grunts, creaks, and squeaks as her mother.

The young killer whale also learns to stay close to the pod. This means the calf doesn't have to use as much energy to push through the water. By following the big killer whales, the calf can just slip along behind them. Swimming among the pod also helps keep the calf safe. While she's small, she could become prey for other predators, such as big sharks.

When the young killer whale is about three years old, the pod begins teaching her how to catch prey. At first, she shares whatever role her mother plays in a hunt and mimics whatever moves her mother makes.

One member of the pod catches a ray. But she lets it go again right in front of the calf so the calf can practice catching it.

By the time the young killer whale is five years old, she's ready to learn the most daring hunting strategy of all. She watches as her mother surges through the surf to snatch a seal off the beach.

The young hunter chases a seal into the surf. But when she feels the stony sand under her belly, she panics. If she gets stuck on the sand, her skin will dry out, her body will overheat, and she'll die. She swerves back into deeper water.

Over and over, the young killer whale chases seals into the surf. Each time, she stops before she reaches shore. But each time, she follows the seal a little farther.

Finally, the young female goes all the way onto the beach, opens her big jaws, and grabs the seal. She's learned how to catch prey onshore, but she's stranded. She squeaks and trills. Her mother swims closer, calling to her.

As the next wave crashes onto her back, the young female wiggles and flops. These movements free her, and she swims with her mother back into deep water. Carrying her prey in her mouth, she takes it to share with the other members of the pod. With this successful hunt, the killer whale hunting family is one generation stronger.

Looking Back

- Check out the killer whales' tails on page 4. Like you, killer whales have backbones, but no bones extend into their tails. A whale's tail is like a rubber paddle that the killer whale moves up and down to propel itself through the water.

- Take another look at the killer whale's tongue on page 10. Like you, the killer whale can wiggle the tip of its tongue. And, like your tongue, the killer whale's tongue is covered with taste buds.

- Look closely at the killer whale's eye on page 19. A killer whale is much bigger than a cow, but its eyes are about the size of a cow's eyes. Special glands at the corners of the killer whale's eyes produce an oily, jellylike substance that coats the eyes to keep them clean and able to move freely.

Glossary

BLOWHOLE: the opening on top of a killer whale's head through which it breathes

BLUBBER: fat that forms a thick layer under a whale's skin. Blubber helps the whale keep warm in cold seawater.

BREACHING: leaping out of the water

CALF: a baby killer whale

DORSAL FIN: the tall fin extending from a killer whale's back

ECHOES: sounds that are reflected, or bounced back

EYE: a body part that detects reflected light rays and sends signals to the brain so an animal can see

FLUKE: the broad tail fin that a killer whale moves up and down to propel itself forward or launch itself upward

ICE FLOE: a floating chunk of ice

POD: a group of killer whales

PREDATORS: animals that hunt and eat other animals in order to survive

PREY: an animal that a predator catches to eat

SCHOOL: a large group of fish

SPYHOPPING: a whale pushing its head out of the water to look around

More Information

BOOKS

Baird, Robin. *Killer Whales of the World: Natural History and Conservation.* Stillwater, MN: Voyageur Press, 2002. Chapters provide details on behavior and the basic biology of killer whales. The book also explores human interactions with killer whales.

Le Bloas, Renee, and Jerome Julienne. *The Orca: Admiral of the Sea.* Watertown, MA: Charlesbridge Publishing, 2001. This book investigates the language and lives of killer whales.

Morton, Alexandra. *Listening to Whales: What the Orcas Have Taught Us.* New York: Ballantine Books, 2002. Morton is a killer whale researcher and shares more than twenty years of experience studying these fascinating animals.

VIDEOS

Killer Whales of the Pacific Northwest (Superior Promotions, Inc., 2001). Join a killer whale watching tour to view these animals in action.

National Geographic's Killer Whales: Wolves of the Sea (National Geographic, 1993). This film, narrated by David Attenborough, provides a close-up look at killer whales working together to capture prey. It also explores their other behaviors.

Ocean Wilds: Realm of the Killer Whales (Warner Home Video, 2001). The film follows killer whales in the Pacific Northwest as they hunt for herring and salmon.

Index

birth, 22–23
blowhole, 12, 23, 38
blubber, 25, 38
brain, 5, 17, 38
breaching, 7, 14, 15, 16, 38
breathing, 11, 19, 23, 25, 38

calves, 22–30, 38
clicks, 5, 6, 14, 19, 38
coloring, 8, 19

dorsal fin, 20, 38

ears, 5
echoes, 5, 38
eyes, 6, 14, 38

flukes (tails), 9, 18, 38

herring, 18

ice floes, 6, 8, 9, 38

jaws, 5, 15, 35

lungs, 19

mating, 20
milk, 25

nipples, 25
nursing, 25, 26

play, 16
pods, 4, 8, 12, 13, 14, 15, 18, 19, 20, 26, 29, 30, 36, 38
predators, 2, 4, 8, 11, 14, 15, 18, 19, 29, 33, 38
prey, 2, 4, 5, 6, 10, 13, 14, 15, 18, 29, 30, 35, 36, 38

rays, 30

seals, 5, 6, 8, 9, 11, 13, 14, 15, 32, 33, 35
senses, 5, 33, 14
sharks, 5, 29
sleep, 17
sounds, 5, 14, 19, 26, 35, 38
speed, 2, 7, 11, 25
spyhopping, 6, 38
stomach, 19
swimming, 7, 8, 12, 14, 17, 23, 29, 35, 36

teeth, 10, 26
throat, 19, 35
tubes, 19

With love, for my mother, Dorothy Haldeman

The author would like to thank Dr. Ingrid Visser of Orca Research Trust (<www.orcaresearch.org>) for sharing her expertise and enthusiasm. As always, a special thanks to Skip Jeffery, for his help and support.

Photo Acknowledgments

The images in this book are used with the permission of: © David B. Fleetham/Seapics.com, p. 1; © Jasmine Rossi/Seapics.com, pp. 3, 15, 34, 37; © Chris Newbert/Minden Pictures, p. 4; © Ingrid Visser/Seapics.com, pp. 5, 9, 13, 31; © Robert L. Pitman/Seapics.com, p. 6; © Tom Brakefield/CORBIS, p. 7; © Thomas Learned, p. 8; © OSF/T. Martin/Animals Animals, p. 10; © Galen Rowell/CORBIS, p. 11; © Stuart Westmorland/CORBIS, p. 12; © Gerard Lacz/Animals Animals, pp. 16, 24, 27; © Amos Nachoum/Seapics.com, pp. 17, 19; © Brandon D. Cole/CORBIS, p. 21; © Finn Larsen/Ursus Photography, p. 22; © Bev Ford/Ursus Photography, p. 23; © John K. B. Ford/Ursus Photography, pp. 28, 33; © Hiroya Minakuchi/Seapics.com, p. 32.

Front cover: © COLE-V&W/Bruce Coleman Inc. Back cover: Amos Nachoum/Seapics.com.

Carolrhoda Books, Inc.
A division of Lerner Publishing Group
241 First Avenue North
Minneapolis, MN 55401

Website address: www.lernerbooks.com

Library of Congress Cataloging-in-Publication Data

Markle, Sandra.
  Killer whales / by Sandra Markle.
    p.   cm. — (Animal predators)
  Summary: Presents information on the physical characteristics, life cycle, and behavior of killer whales, with an emphasis on how they hunt.
  Includes bibliographical references (p.).
  ISBN: 1−57505−728−X (lib. bdg. : alk. paper)
  1. Killer whale—Juvenile literature. [1. Killer whale. 2. Whales.] I. Title. II. Series.
  QL737.C432M325 2004
  599.53'6—dc22   2003025944

Manufactured in the United States of America
1 2 3 4 5 6 − DP − 09 08 07 06 05 04